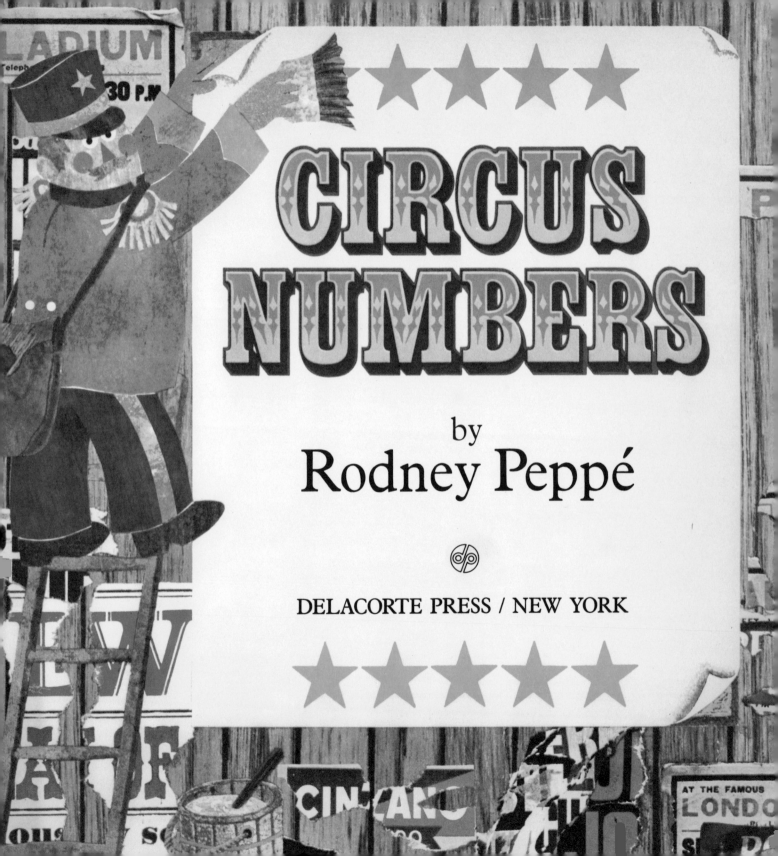

CIRCUS NUMBERS

by
Rodney Peppé

DELACORTE PRESS / NEW YORK

For Jonathan

Published by
Delacorte Press
1 Dag Hammarskjold Plaza
New York, N.Y. 10017

Manufactured in the United States of America

One Previous Edition

New Edition
  First printing

Library of Congress Cataloging in Publication Data

The Library of Congress has cataloged the first
printing of this title as follows:
Peppé, Rodney.
Circus numbers; a counting book. [1st American ed.] New
York, Delacorte Press [1969]
[32] p. (chiefly col. illus.) 24 cm. 3.95
Summary: The performers in the circus ring increase in number from one
to ten.

[1. Counting]   I. Title.
PZ7.P4212Ci   [E]   75-86381
ISBN 0-385-29424-7   MARC
Library of Congress   70[8410]84 rev   AC

This way
to the
Big Tent

We're going to the Circus!

CIRCUS

1

One Ringmaster

2

Two Horses

3

Three Elephants

4

Four Jugglers

5

Five Strongmen

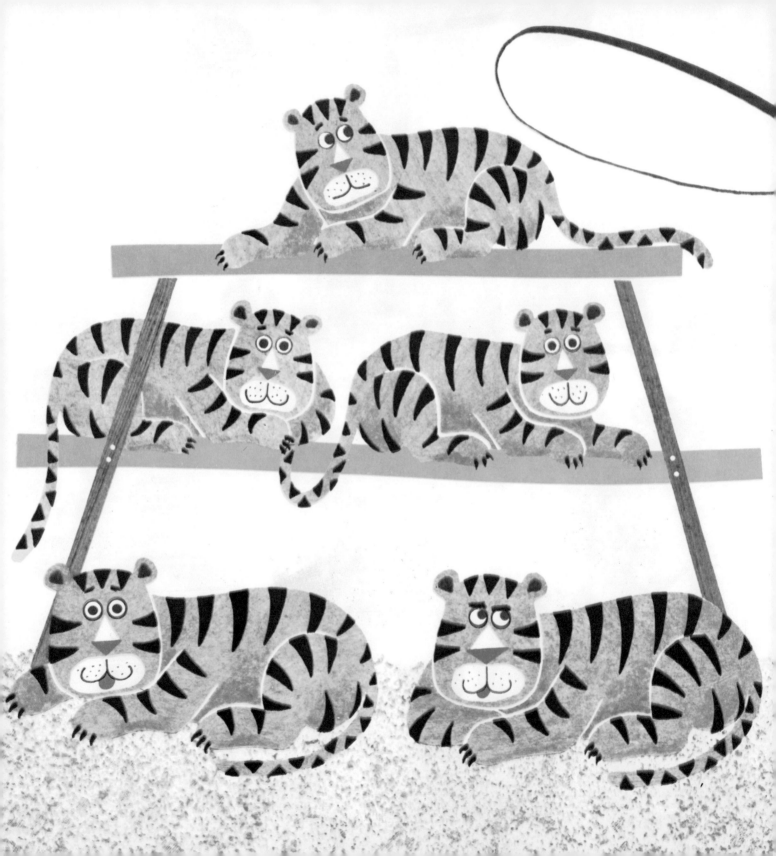

6

Six Tigers

7

Seven Acrobats

8

Eight Seals

9

Nine Bandsmen

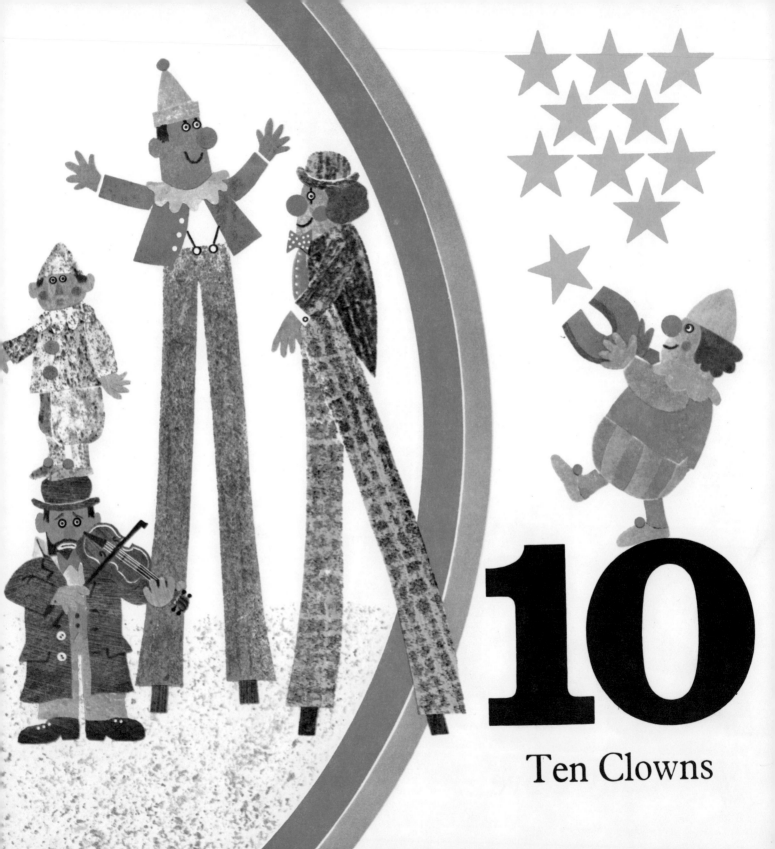

10

Ten Clowns

20
Twenty Doves

100

One Hundred Elephants!

How many . . .

. . . People?

Good-bye

DATE DUE